NO PLACE LIKE DOME!!

A Syracuse and National Cartoon Retrospective

by Joe Glisson

With Much Respect To
Murray Tinkelman

Artist, Teacher, Photographer, Author, Historian,
Mentor, Friend, and National Treasure...
The Cross-Hatch Kid.

For so many of us who have bundled ourselves to journey across campus on a cold Winter's night or spent a late Summer evening wondering 'why didn't air conditioning come with that naming rights deal'... The Dome has a special place in our hearts. While many have written eloquently on the stars and games under the Teflon tent in the corner of my beautiful alma mater, there is just something special about a cartoon. Growing up in New York City I remember opening the sports pages of the Daily News to see the cartoons which captured the story of the day. It takes a special person to in one scene, with few if any words, add perspective and capture the mood of an entire fan base. Game after game, season after season, Joe Glisson has done just that. His creativity and talent have left a collection to remember younger days, sad days and glory days. For those of us who have shed an Orange tinged tear or have a memory of a magic moment from a 'Cuse classic, we treasure this collection of Joe's talents. It truly does remind us that "There's No Place Like Dome!"

—Mike Tirico
ABC & ESPN Sports

10

11

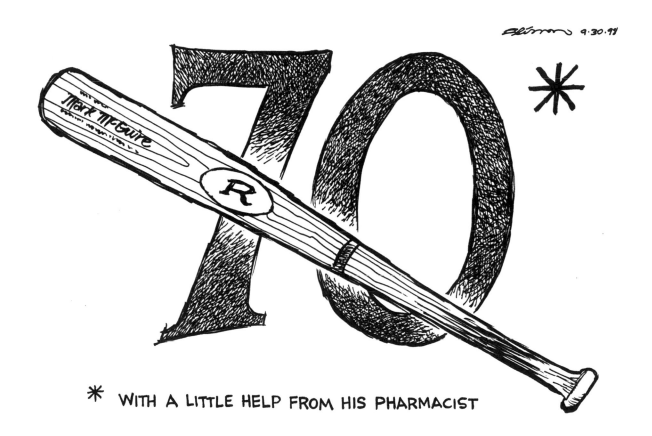

* WITH A LITTLE HELP FROM HIS PHARMACIST

"STAY IN SCHOOL"
1999 POSTER CHILD

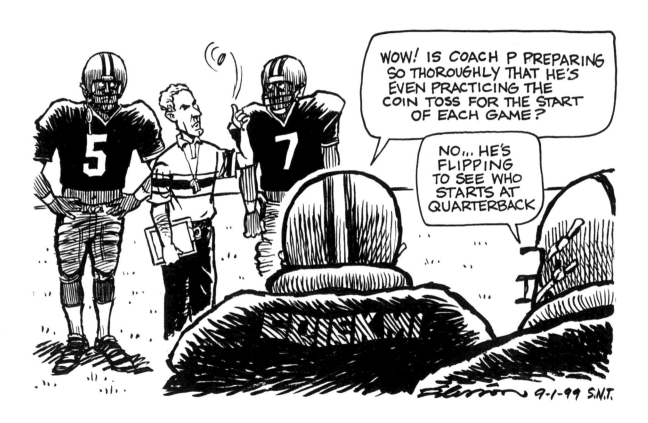

WELL...WE ALWAYS WANTED A PROGRAM OF PENN STATE'S CALIBER...NOW WE GOT ONE: THEY'RE 3-5, AND WE'RE 3-4!!

WITH THE WAY THE JUDGES VOTE, THEY SHOULD CALL IT **GO FIGURE!** SKATING

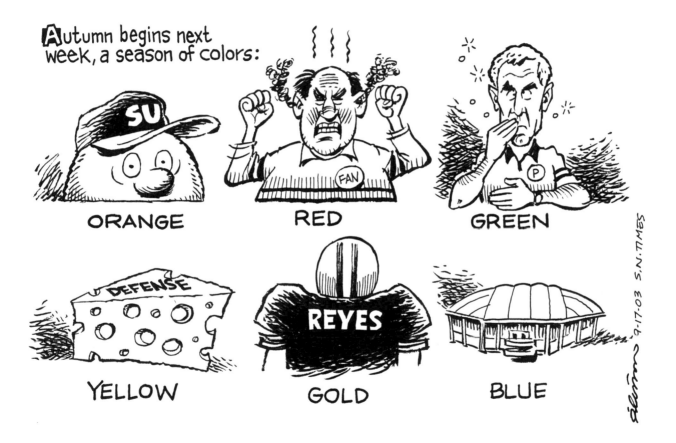

Autumn begins next week, a season of colors:

ORANGE

RED

GREEN

YELLOW

GOLD

BLUE

MID-
SEASON
FORM

ERLAST

POST-
SEASON
FORM

3-10-04 S.N.TIMES

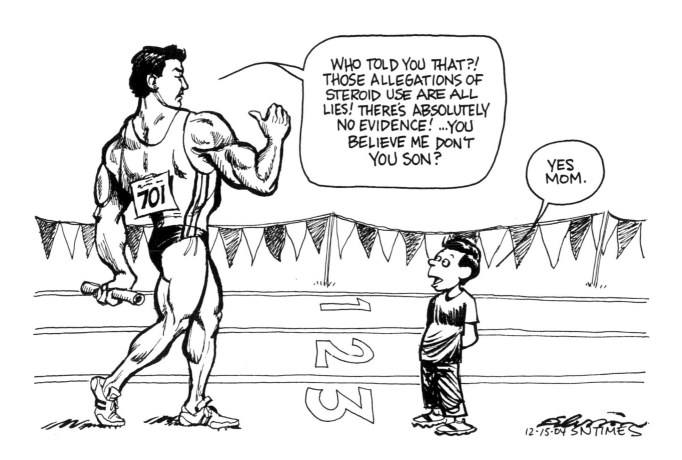

2-16-05 S.N. TIMES

VIVE LE LANCE!

YEP... JUST A LITTLE HOLE YOU'VE DUG FOR YOURSELF. DON'T DIG ANY DEEPER OR YOU JUST MAY NEED IT FOR A **FOXHOLE!**

11-1-06 SYRACUSE N.Y.

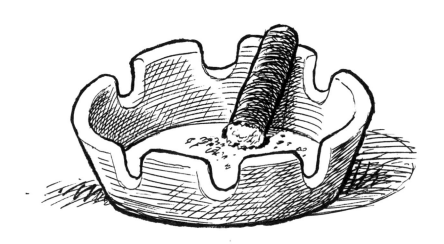

RED AUERBACH
1917 ☘ 2006

3-14-07 S.N. TIMES

LOOKING TO MOVE FASTER OVER LONG DISTANCES THIS YEAR, SANTA DECIDES TO GO WITH THE FAYETTEVILLE-MANLIUS GIRLS CROSS COUNTRY TEAM

SO DOUG... HOW DO YOU LIKE YOUR NEW OFFICE ??

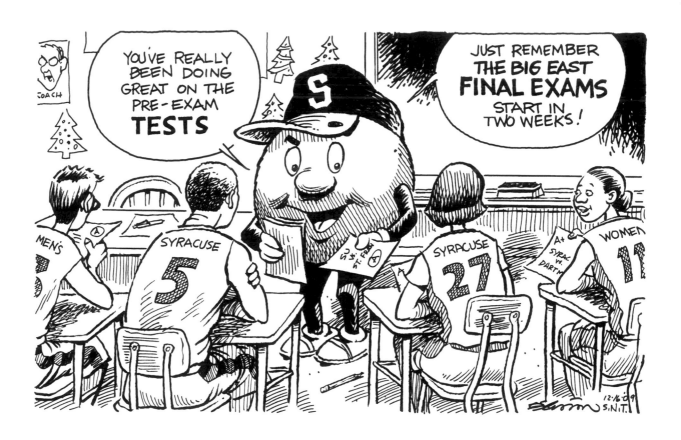

HAPPY BIRTHDAY JAMIE

RED
PARTON

1919 – 2010

136

FLOYD LITTLE SCORES ON HIS LONGEST RUN

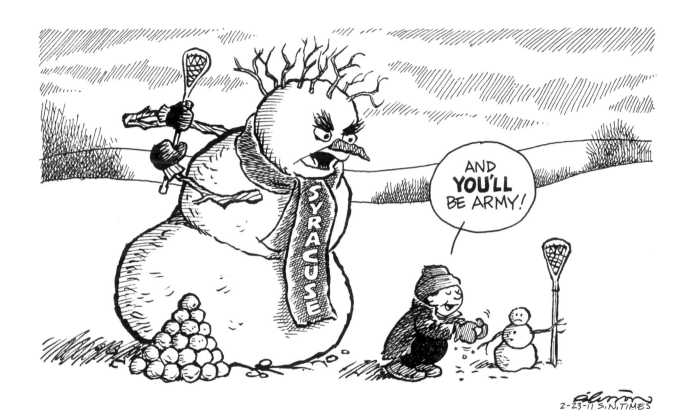

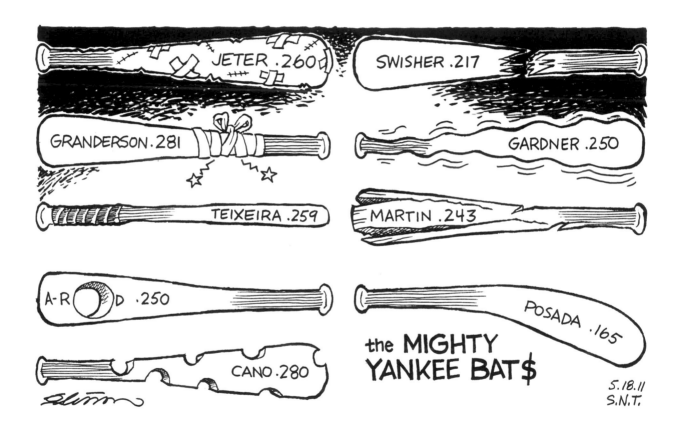

WELCOME
HOME
FLOYD!

SU JOB

A LITTLE GOES A LONG WAY.

6-7-11 S.N.TIMES

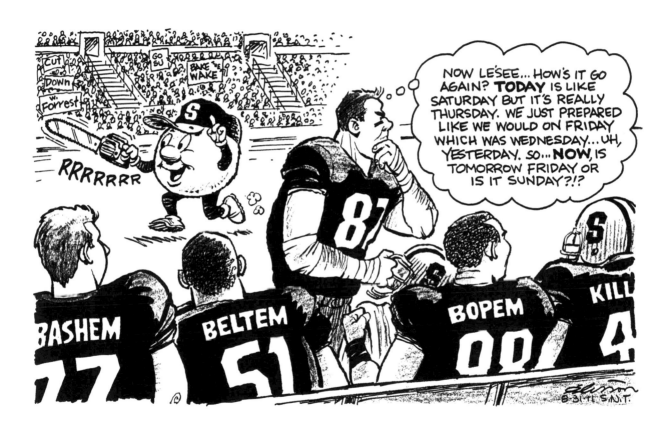

157

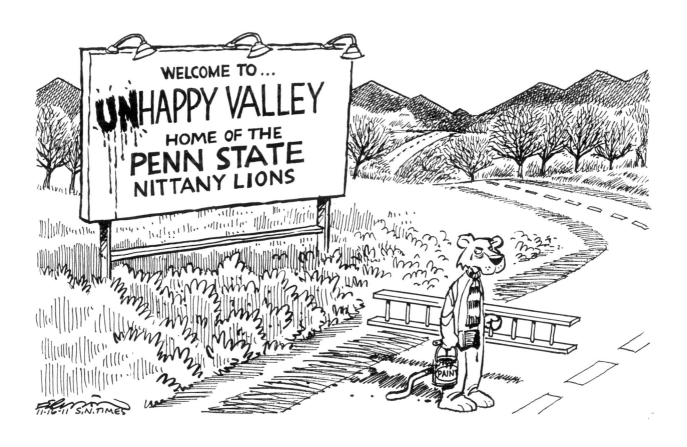

KNIGHT 902 SMITH 879 RUPP 876

163

1-25-12 SYRACUSE NEW TIMES

JOE PATERNO
1926-2012

Proud Supporter of
Syracuse Sports

 Join our Email
Club for special

  Like us!

 Follow us!

www.tullysgoodtimes.com